Life in the PAST LANE

John Steinbuch

Nom de Plume de Bill Burleigh

LIFE IN THE PAST LANE
Thoughts, Aphorisms, Whatever

Bill Burleigh
Founder, Big Sur International
Marathon and Judge (Retired) Assesses
Old Age and other stuff

Illustrated by Shell Fisher

Produced by Alix Lynn Bosch
Additional layout by Kevin Smith,
Pixels Graphic Design
"Go Pixels!" -Bill

ISBN - 13: 978-1-945357-02-2

LIFE IN THE PAST LANE
Thoughts, Aphorisms, Whatever

A small book about aging and other stuff

by John Steinbeck
(Nom de Plume de Bill Burleigh)

- First Edition -
(Very Valuable)

HIGH PRAISE FOR PAST LANE

This is a very, very good book, believe me. And I know books. Better than authors and critics. I haven't had time to read much of this book, but it is very good. But not as good as my book, *The Making of the Deal*. And you can get my book at Amazon for only $19.95, and they will take off a dollar if you mention this book. I just started to read my book and it is excellent.

Donald J. Trump
President of the United States

I am the author; I wrote all the words. Words are the most important part of a book. Past Lane was created by three very old farts. I am the baby at 84; the great illustrator, Shell fisher, is 86; the *Grand Dame* who made it all happen, Elayne Fitzpatrick, is 93. (She forgot to grow old.) That is 265 years of experience. So it has to be good, right? And worthy of another Pulitzer, right?

Bill Burleigh
Author, Past Lane

I am the author's wife. He asked me to edit the book and take out all the bad stuff. That is why this book is so small. What is left, though, is very good. Especially the parts about me. I hope this is Bill's last book. I'm too old for this stuff.

Anne Burleigh
Author's wife

I am the author's oldest daughter. I have known him for 52 years, which is long enough. I live in Egypt now. My Dad sent me this book and asked me to write something nice about it. I read it this morning on the way to work and it is a very good book. I'm not quite sure what his point is, but he does keep your attention. I'm going to give it to a lot of my Arab friends to give them an idea of what very old Americans are like.

Amery Burleigh
Author's daughter

I am the author's Carmel daughter Andee. I am a dog trainer, a positive reinforcement dog trainer, so of course I will praise this book! Praise is my forte!

Good book Dad! Very, very Good Book! Genius! Good Dad!" You get a treat! Many clicks for the chapter on dogs!

If you do not know what it means to click, you need to get a dog and sign up for my classes. Your dog will thank you!

Even if you do not get a dog, SIT! STAY! And READ this book and then praise my dad!

Andee Burleigh
Author's Carmel Daughter

WHAT'S AHEAD

LIFE IN THE PAST LANE

Thoughts, Aphorisms, Whatever

by Bill Burleigh, 84

Take one or two at bedtime, as needed, with or without food.

PREAMBLE

Since retiring I've been jotting down some quirky, occasionally provocative, thoughts. Here they are. I think they're original, at least in presentation.

A good place to keep this book is in your bathroom; lots of little uncomplicated readings. You do not have to think or use much time.

If you don't read this book your life will be empty, hollow and meaningless, without substance, and devoid of wisdom. So there.

chapter 1

AGING:
GROWING UP, OUT, AND DOWN

WEIGHT CONTROL FOR AGING

There is a little calorie-burning furnace in your body called metabolism. I think it's in your left shoulder. As you age it gets tired and inefficient, and doesn't burn calories like it used to. So those little unburnt calories go to the most comfortable place in your body, your tummy.   When that is full, they go to any place they want to. What this means is that you can't keep swallowing calories without dire consequences: FAT!!! As you age, start eating smaller portions of healthy food. Cut back on high calorie things like sweets and oil. Booze is okay in moderation. If you, at the age of

70, ate the same calories you ate when you were 20, you would weigh 427 lbs. Fodder for the Big Nap.

. . . .

When you go to a restaurant, and you have a companion, split one entree; restaurants expect it from seniors. Or, if you are by yourself, take half of it home.

. . . .

Old age is like weed: you lose your short term memory.

. . . .

Some old folks, to quote Dylan Thomas, "... go gentle into that good night.", they just wither and disappear. Others, "Rage, rage against the dying of the light." I count myself one of the latter group. We "Ragers" want to stay relevant. So we work for the community, or write about everything, or learn how to paint, take pictures, sing, *anything to be noticed.* I am even growing a pony tail. The desire to be relevant is one of the reasons I am writing this. I don't want to become a non-person.

. . . .

My skin keeps sliding down. I wonder, if I live long enough, will it fall off?

. . . .

There are four things you need for a long, healthy life: 1. Good genes, 2. Exercise, 3. Nutrition, 4. Involvement in the community.

· · · · · · · · · · ·

I'm like a car. I think I compare favorably with a '52 Chevy Twice Pipe: classic style but a little tired and no longer a Chick Magnet. My upholstery is almost completely worn out, and the only working electronic device is the radio. The engine is okay as long as I regularly change the merlot. My transmission and exhaust system need a little work. I think I will keep on going for another 50,000 miles before being relegated to the junk yard.

. . . .

It is normal, as we age, to be holding some object, put it down and then not be able to find it. In our sixties, we would lose things in the house, in the seventies we lose things in a room, in our eighties it can be in a bed: the cap to your pen, the remote, a hearing aid, a cookie, your Viagra.

. . . .

I accidentally looked at myself in the mirror the other day. I don't know how it happened, but I have someone else's arms.

One nice thing about aging is that an ounce of whiskey will give you a narcotic effect. And that is, after all, the only reason we drink alcohol, isn't it? Would you drink vodka, gin, etc., if they had no alcohol?

LIFE IS GOOD!

JUDICIAL DISCRETION

You might have noticed that Judges do not put people over 80 in jail. Here's why:

Robber, 85; *"This is a stick up! Your money or your... uh...your... help me with this!*

Minimart clerk: *"Life"*

Robber: *"Right. Your money or your life!"*

Clerk: *"Sir, your gun is not real."*

Robber: *"Of course it isn't. If I could afford a real gun I wouldn't be doing this."*

. . . .

    I just realized that it is impossible for me to suffer an untimely demise. Also I noticed that I have passed my use-by date.

. . . .

    You might be getting old if you call your cell phone more than a couple times a day to find out where it is.

My children were visiting recently, and I mentioned to them that it would be a good idea to show them where I keep my important documents, my passwords and how to fix things that are unique to my property -- and things that need to be done if something happens to me. They were way too enthusiastic about learning this stuff.

The basic laws of physics prove that objects grow heavier as years go by. And print grows smaller, and hills get steeper and light bulbs grow dimmer, and people get taller, and your friends don't articulate anymore. Driving lanes get narrower, and the person next to you at the table has a higher chair. Your old computer is much harder to operate. All this happens as we get older. Must be a coincidence.

. . . .

Dim eyesight has an upside: the carpet is always clean and you don't see ticks or fleas on the dogs.

. . . .

Finger dexterity is one of many things that diminish with age. Texting has gone in the dustbin; keyboard is too small. Tiny pills

disappear. Forget about buttoning
your collar buttons.

· · · · · · · · · · · ·

We don't like making messes
on the table and spilling wine. The
worst messes to clean up are
ground coffee, granulated sugar,
and red wine. If you are lucky
enough to reach old age, you will
drop food on your clothes and spill
wine.

· · · · · · · · · · · ·

Take heed: if you wear dark
clothing and walk or ride a bike
beside the road, in the shade, you
are invisible to most of us old folks.

· · · · · · · · · · · ·

My memory has reached the point where anyone can accuse me of doing anything, at any time in the past, and I can't deny it.

. . . .

The road I live on, like most private roads in Big Sur, has an electronic gate. I came back from running an errand, drove up to the gate, and just sat there. Thinking about whatever I was thinking about. It could have been a couple of minutes or more before I returned to reality and pushed the clicker button to open the gate.

. . . .

Young kids say they are older than they are. Middle age people say they are younger than they are. Old men (not women) say they are older than they are. What's with that?

· · · · · · · · · · · ·

Old folks don't get much done because they spend so much time looking for things they lost and cleaning up the messes they make. Like putting spaghetti in the microwave for 16 minutes and not hearing the explosions because you were in the bathroom.

HOVERING MORTALITY

At 84 I am at the age where the Reaper guy could visit at any moment, right? So I figure I'd better start getting ready. I have already had my Memorial Service, which was great fun. I took a selfie yesterday so Anne could have a current photo... and I think I will write my own obituary. People believe everything they read in an obit, so I will slip in things like, "Bill was the first person to fly an ultralight under the Golden Gate Bridge" and "Bill gave away his entire inheritance, over a million dollars. The week he received it he started a home for abandoned puppies." People will read that and say, "Gee, what a wonderful guy he was."

. . . .

People of advanced maturity like me have problems with night driving, or in the rain... so I don't do it anymore. There are some that say I don't do it on a dry day, either.

. . . .

Even seniors have an occasional burst of energy, a need to produce, and get things done that we have been putting off. I had one of those last week, so I went out and put the sticker on my license plate. Then came in for another nap.

. . . .

DISCRIMINATION?

For some reason the infirmities of old age are not given the same dignity as other disabilities, like loss of a leg.

I can't read books and magazines anymore because the print is too small and there is not enough light. But Time magazine keeps reducing its print size, especially for captions. (For those who can afford it, digital books and magazines provide some relief.) Also, if you need to read a paper, put on a head light, an elastic band with a light, and get a magnifying glass. I have one in every room. The glass costs less that $10. (The Center for Disease Control found that 2.9 million Americans have natural vision loss, 9.1 million suffer from Age Related Macular Degeneration, and 2.5 million from diabetic impairment.)

Packages get harder to open, pills get smaller, and devices get more complex, even your three year old iPhone. How about cutting us some slack?

· · · · · · · · · · · ·

Everything in our house, the floors, bedspreads, counters, carpets, etc. has a color that is compatible with coffee. That's because coffee is what I spill, drop or knock over more than any other color.

Another nice thing about getting old is that you are not expected to do anything. Just help clear the table, then go watch the game.

· · · · · · · · · · ·

Oldsters get great gas mileage. We seldom drive over 50 or 60 mph, and we almost never pass. An 80 year old can turn any vehicle into hybrid mileage.

· · · · · · · · · · ·

Someone said that I had one of those new driverless cars, even though I am driving my old sedan.

· · · · · · · · · · ·

Any object an old person picks up is likely to be lost. At least temporarily.

. . . .

If I keep shrinking I won't die; I will just disappear.

. . . .

The reason we have all the plastic packaging of so many things is because of the public's over-reaction to one lousy poisoning of a bottle of aspirin, 60 years ago. In Europe you don't see as much plastic packaging.

. . . .

I would like to live to be 100, but only if my brain lives with me. I'll let someone else take care of my body as long as I am aware and can articulate.

THAT'S ALL, FOLKS

When I'm dead, I'm gone. Don't waste precious time grieving. Go ahead and laugh, sing and dance whenever you feel like it. Find someone else. You will remember me and that is enough. And when you think of me, smile or laugh, just don't cry. (A life size statue of me would be just fine.)

Anne and I, who are 78 and 84, bought Giant Sequoia seedlings. And I bought a new car and 20 pair of boxer shorts and a 10 terabyte back-up hard drive. Is this called whistling in the cemetery?

* * * * * * * * * * * *

My favorite straw hat sits on my ears now. I think my head is shrinking. My brain cells that die are not being replaced as well as before, leaving a hole. Nature abhors a vacuum, so she/he is just squishing my head together.

* * * * * * * * * * * *

The older I get the more emotional I get. Yesterday I cried when my team made a first down. And as soon as the violins play in a movie, my eyes get wet. A good parking place is worth a few tears.

THICK PLASTIC BUBBLE WRAP PACKAGING

Things you should have on hand when starting to open a bubble wrap package from Costco: scissors, shears, box cutter, awl, tin snips, wire cutters, Goo Gone, loppers, pruning saw, chain saw, first aid kit, defibrillator, and ambulance. And, maybe, a hearse.

. . . .

Life is like a flashlight battery. Strong and reliable for a long time, then it starts to fade and get dimmer.

I think in a few years I will have to be replaced. Remember, don't put me in with the regular trash. Too bad I can't be recharged, but you have to believe in a God to get that service.

Maybe it would be better to come back as a house. If I were a house, I could just remodel and update myself every 20 years, and go on forever.

. . . .

Old folks have the wisdom to keep wearing clothes that are tattered but clean, because the old clothes are comfortable and still work.

DISPOSAL SERVICE

When I start the big sleep, I don't want to be cooked in an oven or dumped into a hole in the ground. That's pagan ritual. I would much prefer being dropped into a canyon in Big Sur, and join the food chain. A few meals for a mountain lion would be nice, but I will settle for a coyote, fox or (yuk) a condor. I can hear them, "Wow! This one is really marbled!"

* * * * * * * * * * * *

The discs between your vertebrae are getting squashed as you age, and eventually you will walk stooped or bent over. You can avoid some of this by lifting weights, and following the admonition of a theatre director to his cast: "Tits to the balcony!" Whenever you can remember, keep your shoulders pushed back.

. . . .

We like to visit old friends and relatives that we haven't seen for 20 or 30 years, just to see how bad they look.

. . . .

Old people become non-people to some young people. If you are a grandparent, you are lucky if any of your grandchildren pay any attention to you. But remember, you didn't pay any attention to *your* grandparents.

It is not a good sign that when something is missing, your first reaction is that someone stole it.

· · · · · · · · · · ·

Everything in your body slows down as you age. Including your brain, AKA comprehension. When you are in your eighties, it is hard to read the closed captions on TV before they move on; if your friend talks too fast, you have to say, "'What?" to slow him down. If the plot in a movie is too complicated, you can't follow it. Subtleties go right by you. Reduced comprehension plus dimming eyes cut back on the pleasure of film. What doesn't slow down is time; it just keeps flying by. And there is absolutely nothing you can do about it.

• • • • • • • • • • •

Microwave ovens were invented for old folks who think cooking is too much trouble. You can maintain a healthy life on five minutes of preparation for a meal: frozen veggies, salmon, three berries etc. from Costco; salads, perishables, potatoes, etc. from Safeway. Add a little wine, and Voila! La Dolce Vita! (Here you get mixed languages.)

• • • • • • • • • • •

When you see an oldster moving slowly and deliberately when he goes around a corner or puts an object on the table, you may think that he is under the influence. Actually, he is just not sure where his legs or arms will end up. (Then again, maybe he had too much to drink.)

.   .   .   .

The mantra of old folks is "It's too much trouble". That is the common response to "Let's go to a movie" or "Let's go out to dinner" or "Let's take a trip." Sometimes it is even too much trouble to get into trouble.

.   .   .   .

If I say "disable" to my wife, when I meant to say "decanter", she will know what I mean. Old married folks usually know what the other one is saying. We often refer to things we can't remember the name of, as thingies. And we know what we mean.

. . . .

If I am late meeting you, take it easy on me. I had to go back to the house from the car four times before I left, to get my keys, then glasses, then dark glasses, etc.

. . . .

Old folks don't think they are old. They just look and act old.

Beware of the area behind a car with a geezer driving. Sometimes we are so stiff it is too hard to turn around to look behind. So we just back up until we hit something.

I am losing so many nouns due to aging, that I think I will take the course called English as a Second Language.

LIFE IS TERRIFIC

Fast is past. Express lanes on the freeway are history to the elderly. What we old timers need is to make the far right lane on a big freeway a slow lane, speed limit of 50.

. . . .

Bumper stickers on cars are a waste of time for old folks. We can't get close enough to read them.

. . . .

Official song for old folks, that great hit from the 40s: "Try to remember...."

. . . .

We used to check the house to turn out lights when we went to bed. Now we don't have to because it is still daylight.

· · · · · · · · · · ·

To remove the plastic protective sleeve for the top of a tiny bottle of over-the-counter medication, like eye drops, requires a box cutter and a steady hand. I have a box cutter.

· · · · · · · · · · ·

Old age must be intoxicating; I keep passing out on the couch.

· · · · · · · · · · ·

The only way an old guy can see all those pesky little hairs on his face, ears and nose, is if they are on fire.

. . . .

Thermostats don't work for the aged; older is colder. Eighty degrees is the new seventy. Global warming got here just in time.

. . . .

The hair on top of my head slid down to my ears and nostrils.

. . . .

If you have a puppy, don't leave your hearing aids on the coffee table.

. . . .

If it weren't for seniors, AAA would not need a roadside assistance program. Last year I locked my keys in the car, and the AAA guy arrived, put his hand through the back window I had left half open for the dog, and opened the door. Recently Anne locked her keys in her car. We both tried to use the emergency key but couldn't make it work. So we had AAA drive a big truck for an hour to get to us, and he put the same key in and opened the door.

* * * * * * * * * * * *

If you are reading this, you woke up this morning. That is

enough to have yourself a fine day.

. . . .

How many seniors does it take to change a light bulb in the ceiling? None. If someone won't do it for us, we will do without it.

HEAR, HEAR

There are fifth and sixth strings on a guitar, a brush on a drum makes a fine rhythm for a ballad, and a triangle complements an orchestra. Things do go bump in the night, and cereal really does go snap, crackle and pop. I made all these (re)discoveries when I got my hearing aids a few years ago. If you decide to get a hearing aid, here is a hint: I got mine half price by getting them off a cadaver. (You know, used.)

· · · · · · · · · · ·

For the elderly, dinnertime and bed time are almost indistinguishable.

· · · · · · · · · · ·

Message to the young from the old: we move slowly because our extremities don't always do what we tell them to. We lose about 1% of our body strength each year after 40. We can slow the rate by lifting weights and walking/running, but nature gets us all. Someday you will not be able to do the things that need strength. I can look at a rung in a ladder and miss it by half an inch. We deal with it, so you have to take us as we are. You tolerate us and we'll tolerate you.

. . . .

A couple hundred years ago when I was in college, there was a popular song in drinking ev1ents that went: "My eyes are dim, I cannot see…" I assumed that dimness was caused by alcohol. Now I don't need alcohol.

. . . .

There should be a monument to Big Pharma. Without pills you wouldn't have very many friends over 75. The companies would not create new drugs if you took out the profit. It is a business, but we owe them thanks anyway.

· · · · · · · · · · ·

I keep telling myself, think of all the things I remembered today. So what if I forgot a few things.

· · · · · · · · · · ·

I wanted to talk to my son-in-law and gave Anne a phone to dial the number for me. But I accidentally gave her the TV remote. She looked at it for at least five seconds, trying to figure out how to dial it.

. . . .

My dogs hang around whenever I am eating something; they expect me to drop some of it. When I do, they clean it up better than I could, for which I am eternally grateful.

. . . .

I lose about 20 - 30 nouns every week or so. (I think they fall out my nose.) Wouldn't it be awful if we lost verbs?

LIFE IS WONDERFUL!

My horizontal movement has gone from run to walk to shuffle to lurch.

· · · · · · · · · · · ·

I used to be Anne's Trophy Husband. Now I am her Rescue Person. She feeds me (I get to lick her plate) and makes sure I get my shots and pills, and I get to sleep in her bed.

· · · · · · · · · · · ·

Nested coffee filters are a conspiracy to get old folks, who can't see or feel, to use three or four at a time.

· · · · · · · · · · · ·

My left ear and left eyeball have pretty much faded into history, but it is no problem. I have a spare set on the right. Is that why nature gave us two of so many things?

chapter 2

DOGS: AT ONCE, THE SMALLEST AND BIGGEST THINGS IN YOUR LIFE

We shrink when we age. I wonder if dogs shrink as they age. I guess I could google it but it is too much trouble.

. . . .

One dog is fun and loving. Two dogs are ten times more fun and loving. Three dogs are ten dogs, and less fun .

. . . .

If your dog didn't sniff your crotch, who would?

. . . .

Dogs do not drink alcohol. That is why there are no dog alcoholics. Or dog DUI's.

Everybody wants to be loved. This morning I was reading in bed when Taylor Swift, my 20lb male terrier mix, plopped down against my shoulder. He looked up at me, wagged his tale, tried to lick my chin, and kicked with his hind legs to get closer. I tickled his tummy and he stuck his nose in my armpit. All of this made me feel good. I wonder if I could get my wife to do these things.

Nothing feels better to touch than the skin of the person you love. Or the fur of the animal you love.

. . . .

I like dogs so much I am beginning to act like them. I just lay around the house all day.

. . . .

I trained my dog to do the normal tricks, like sit, stay, roll over, play dead and beg. Then I taught him to ignore the commands.

. . . .

Your health is more important than your family, friends, job and everything else in life except your *dog*.

THEY COMPENSATE

I have a wonderful little dog that is lovable, playful and an almost total delight. A couple times a month he pees on the floor; I tried for half a year to train him but he just can't control his bladder. I love him so much I quit scolding him and accept his problem. I also told Anne that I loved her so much she could pee on the floor.

It's nice, polite, and appreciated to acknowledge people's arrival, even if they have only been away a few hours. Your dog can teach you how to do it.

- - - - - - - - - - - -

If you gave everyone in the world a gentle, loving dog, and the means to take care of it, there would be no wars or organized religion. A small percentage of recipients would abandon or eat their dogs, but the world would still be a better place.

Chapter 3

RELATIONSHIPS:
HOW TO MAKE FRIENDS, MALE
AND FEMALE, AND KEEP THEM

The single most important thing in any relationship - family, political, employment, etc. - is HARMONY. If you can just remember that, and always try for it, your life will be much happier. So when you get angry, or want to criticize, or feel like raising your voice, remember: harmony.

· · · · · · · · · · ·

An important characteristic for life, which we badly need when we are younger but don't normally get until we are older, is the ability to say "no". You used to say yes to an evening with another couple that bore you to tears, but now you can say, "Sorry, we are busy"..... and work mates that want to share gifts for some holiday, buy something the neighbor made, or read a book to please a writer... (you obviously ignored that since you are reading this.) "Remember, life is finite and sometimes it is okay to be selfish. As long as you are still polite.

* * * * * * * * * * *

Nobody appreciates you as much as you do ~ Nobody can bathe you as well as you can ~ Nobody is as critical of you as you are ~ Only you can embarrass yourself ~ You are the only one who doesn't know what you look like to others ~ You are the only one who cannot see all your flaws ~ You are the only one who

knows the intensity of your
insecurity.

. . . .

My wife Anne and I have had
enough experience to appreciate
each other... i.e., we are tolerant of
almost everything in our partner.

There are only two necessary
ingredients to a successful, lasting
marital relationship: you have to
respect each other, and there has to
be enough money. If either of those
is missing, the marriage is probably
doomed. Other ingredients, like
harmony, love, affection, sex,
ambition, humor, health, religion,
integrity, music, generosity,
sensitivity, gentleness, are all great,

but they are just icing on the cake and the marriage can survive without them.

. . . .

A woman's intuition is usually right. For no reason at all.

. . . .

A lot of people are uncomfortable in social settings. That is because we all have to perform when in that setting, and we are concerned that our performance may not pass muster. Socializing is hard work, sometimes exhausting.

. . . .

The only advice my father ever gave me was, be tolerant and take your vices in moderation. I've never forgotten that and I have tried to honor that advice.

Sometimes it is very hard. I thought I was smoking in moderation until I tried to quit. It took six attempts, and during one of them I was driving across town and had to pull over and weep.

Are you moderate in your work, sex, drinking, smoking, exercise, eating, speech, etc.? Are you tolerant of people who are not moderate?

GODS

My parents took me to church during my intellectually formative years. When I was about 16, my mother asked what I thought about religion. I said it didn't make much sense to me, and she said she agreed. The preacher would say that God loved me so much he killed his only son, or a virgin gave birth, or what the Bible says is true, and I would think, what's with that? So... I have been an atheist all my life. (I think they have softened that word to "Humanist") I'm not proud or ashamed of it. I just can't believe in anything based solely on faith. (Although I have problems with what makes a baby's heart start beating, or why I fell permanently in love with my wife and Big Sur in five minutes.)

· · · · · · · · · · · ·

I think organized religion has done a lot of harm to humanity, and there is a lot of factual support for that conclusion. But, all in all, it has probably done more good than harm. Faith gives people peace of mind, and a way to face inhumanities and death. And without the enormous financial success of religion, particularly Catholic sponsors, I wonder if we would have had a Michelangelo, Da Vinci, St. Peter's Basilica, et al. And churches have always been good about helping orphans and the homeless. (Government should but often won't).

FIND A PARTNER

If you are single and don't want to be, get on the internet. It may take a couple years online, but there is someone out there who will love you as much as you love them. I can say from experience that it is WONDERFUL. At any age.

SEX

Nature gave us animals a dose of testosterone (lust) to keep the species alive. We have taken what nature gave us, horniness, to great heights, with enormous imagination and great joy. For some inexplicable reason, there are people who are embarrassed or even against sex. There is absolutely no reason for that. Sex should be fun! If anyone (a preacher?) says it is bad, ask them why. They will not have a factual reason to support their opinion... just opinions... and, perhaps, the Bible, or Koran, books that were written by old white men, not one woman in the bunch.

We don't drink water, eat food, or breathe air unless we think it is safe, and we need to give the same dignity to sex: don't get a disease or create an unwanted child, or participate in sex when you are too young to know how important it is.

So, here is the starting point: you must know sex is safe. Once that is covered, go for it: With gusto if you both feel like it. (Respect for your partner is a must; love is a great bonus) Laugh, sing, paint bodies, design with the magic marker, masturbate, get out the Hitachi Wand vibrator, (Wanda, who I just realized is old enough to vote!) do anything you both want to, *if nobody gets hurt.* (Rumor has it that the value of vibration was discovered when operators of jack hammers kept ejaculating.) Orgasms feel as great at 80 as at 20, even if aided by the vibrator. My vibrator has calluses. (Men: you don't need an erection to have an orgasm.) There is one last caveat, as John Lennon said, don't frighten the horses.

SEX IS WONDERFUL!

VALUE OF BREVITY

Any comment made to one or more people in conversation, such as in a bar or coffee shop or family gathering, should never exceed one minute. In those environments no listener has an attention span longer than one minute; eyes glaze over.

No Statement in this book takes more than one minute to read. Same for jokes: never go more than a minute. Sample: Putin walks in to a bar, and the bartender says, "What can I get you?" and he says, "Ukraine". Another: A blonde is driving down the freeway when her husband calls: "Honey, you have to be careful, I just saw on TV that a car is going the wrong way on the freeway!" "They all are!" Last and best: Two beets are walking down the road when a car hits one of them. They take him to the hospital, and the doctor comes out and says to the other beet in the waiting room, "I have good news and bad news. The good news is that your friend will survive. The bad news is that for the rest of his life he will be a vegetable."

FLAWED PEOPLE

I have read a lot of biographies, and have come to the conclusion that everyone is flawed. You are only allowed 11 flaws; after that you should be put away. Our favorite heroes of history like Teddy Roosevelt, Martin Luther King, JFK, FDR, et al, were all very flawed, but not more than 11. Trump is at 64 and doomed. I only have 2, one less than my wife.

WHY DID YOU SAY THAT?

There is no need to criticize, correct or belittle someone, unless it is important, and most things are not important. It serves no purpose if it is not important. It's okay to disagree. Think back about your last few fights with someone: were they important? Pick your fights carefully. If you like to question things and argue (like I do) pick people to fight with that also like to question things and argue. Remember this: MOST PEOPLE LIKE HARMONY. Including my wife.

LGBT

Lesbians, gays, bisexuals and transgenders are a small group of normal people that generally prefer their own sex instead of the opposite sex. Homosexuality can be traced back to an ancient

Egyptian male couple in 2,400 BC. Wikipedia has a lengthy discussion. No one knows what percentage of the human race is homosexual because it is still illegal or considered a sin in many cultures and people are reluctant to identify themselves. In Russia homo-sexuality is illegal, and in the Southern areas, which are mostly Muslim, the government rounds up the LGBT and beats and tortures them, sometimes to death. The percentage of homosexuals in the population is small. One estimate based on considerable research said it was 1.7%, but the authors admitted it was probably much higher. The bottom line though, is this: they do not hurt anybody by reason of their sexual preference. If you hear them criticized, ask what facts they have to support their prejudice. They will have none because there are none.

HATE FOR NO REASON

There would be no wars if people would tolerate conduct that doesn't hurt anybody, like religious beliefs, skin color or sexual choices. (That, my friends, is a very profound statement: toleration rocks).

WE ARE TOO BUSY

It's hard to get four people together for lunch. They have all kinds of commitments, even the old folks. One of the reasons we are too busy is that, as you read this, hundreds of people are writing or preparing articles, books, emails, text messages, movies, etc., that you just have to read or see. Often these things stack up for a long time before you delete or toss them or they are no longer available. And you still feel guilty. And here's the rub: there is absolutely nothing you can do about it.

ABORTION

Abortion has been written about and accepted since the ancient Greeks, 500 B.C. The first outright prohibition came from Christianity, as you might expect, in 140 A.D. Now abortion is in and out of favor in every culture in the world. The penalties have ranged from zero to death. The U.S. had a hodge-podge of states accepting or criminal-izing abortion until 1973, when *Roe v. Wade*, by the Supreme Court, made it nationally legal. There will always be a strong opposition because it is an article of faith; abortion is killing and no amount of factual explanation will change that view.

Life is so much easier if we compromise, even to the point of giving up something important. Stop and think: is it worth losing this relationship by not giving up the issue? No one expects you to give up your core beliefs but most disputes are way below that.

MANNERS PAY BIG DIVIDENDS

Civility and manners are important. You have to treat everyone with respect, *even if they don't deserve it.* You have to say "Thank you, "No thank you", "You're welcome", "Please", "Sorry, and "Can I help", *even if you don't want to and don't mean it.* You have to respond when spoken to. And look people in the eye. If you have good manners it excuses a multitude of sins.

. . . .

You can't control your emotions, like love, anger, joy, depression, etc., but you can control what shows, your outward appearance of the emotion.

DO WE NEED BONES?

The long caravan of luxury hearses was hauling old, torn body parts from a field in Ukraine to

Belgium. They said the best parts were the heads because they had dental records for Id's. We taxpayers spend millions of dollars recovering unquestionably dead bodies from the bottom of the ocean, caves in Guadalcanal and the jungles of Vietnam. When the body part gets home, they say, "Oh, thank you God for bringing him home." Then they bury the body part in the ground. So what's that about? (Maybe it is a female gene connected to nurturing).

GUNS

I've taken on sex, religion,
gays, politics and just about all
things you are supposed to avoid,
so I might as well take on guns. My
position is, of course, unassailable.
You can shoot all the government
agents coming to kill you, or all the
burglars and robbers you can find,
with a shotgun or rifle. The only
reason to have a hand gun is to kill
a human being. That is all they are
good for. You couldn't hit a deer 50
feet away with a pistol. Most illegal
killings by gun are by hand guns.
So, ban all handguns (and machine
guns) except for law enforcement,
military and security personnel.
That was my position when I ran

for President, but NRA gave a zillion dollars to my opponent and I lost.

Someone suggested that we treat guns like vehicles. We acknowledge their legality and importance and recognize their danger. So we register them, regulate them, and track them, like cars.

A Haiku is a Japanese aphorism in three lines:

Energy comes from the Sun

And from Anne's presence

And Anne's touch.

Chapter 4

POLITICS: WHAT WE LOVE TO HATE AND HATE TO LOVE

(Caveat: What follows is some heavy duty stuff. Kind of a Liberal's Manifesto. Not many smiles for a while. Conservatives should read it just to criticize my position.)

PRIVACY

Keep this in mind: everything you say or do publicly could be on the front page of the newspaper, digital or paper, or on radio or TV. That is because everything you say or do publicly is probably being recorded, audio and/or video, by someone... mostly government and business. The only private place you have is within the four walls of your home and the middle of the National Forest. And even those areas are not protected for what you voluntarily send outside by social or business media such as emails, Facebook, Twitter, etc. Those could be on the front page, too. You permanently gave up your privacy when you got your first credit card. So you have to just deal with it.

· · · · · · · · · · ·

Nature does whatever it wants to, with no conscience or apologies; it creates beauty in butterflies and ballet, and disasters in earthquakes and Donald Trump. With no sorrow or joy.

REGULATION NEEDED

There is way too much government regulation of business and individuals, but not near enough regulation of government. Why should the Feds control the sanitation of barber shops in Memphis? But they do, all over the country. Why did the Feds make a small health clinic in Big Sur, CA put insulation in the walls to protect the privacy of patients? These things should be up to the States, or even counties and towns. But the Feds have no laws that penalize them for wasting money, and there is no enforceable law of ethics, with penalties, to keep them in check. Shouldn't there be some regulation and oversight on the amount of vacation time for Federal employees, including Congress, the White House and the judiciary?

GREED (gred)   Noun
Intense and selfish desire for something, especially wealth; excessive or rapacious desire for wealth or possessions. See conservative Republicans. "He (Donald Trump) has an appetite [for property] like a Rocky Mountain vulture." Alan Greenberg, *Wall Street Journal*, April 1, 1987. If a man makes an annual salary of $100 million, and demands of the Board or Team Owner a raise of $10 million or he will leave, that is naked greed.

MONEY AND POLITICS

A major difference between liberals and conservatives is

attitude toward money. The former looks at money as a valuable tool to use. The latter looks at money as something to be saved, not used. Hardline conservatives don't care about government, as long as it makes them wealthier. In order to accumulate money they want low taxes and little money for the poor and disabled because they are "lazy or fraudulent". It is hard for a conservative to admit that poor people don't want to be poor, that they can't get work because there is none, or they don't qualify because of diminished mental ability or health. Liberals favor citizens over business, Conservatives favor business over citizens.

Further discussion of the supreme effect of money. Example: I hope we all agree that the poor and helpless need to be taken care of; they need shelter, food and clothing. Liberals would say government must do it, and get the money from the people who can afford it. E.g., have a minimum tax of $50K for people that make $500k and would not miss the $50K, rather than the people that make $50K, who would be hurt by a loss of $5K.

The conservatives would rather that the community - churches and non-profits take care of the poor and disabled. But if government had to do it, they would rather tax the middle class than the wealthy, calling a tax on the rich the forbidden "income redistribution", (which has been with us since 1913 in the Sixteenth Amendment). The silliest argument they make to protect the rich, is that if we take away their money, they can't hire people. And if we give them a tax cut, the rich will use it to hire people. History shows us those arguments are invalid; if we raise their taxes they don't fire people, they just pass it on to the consumers. When Reagan and Bush cut taxes on the rich, unemployment went up, as well as the deficit.

HARD QUESTION

This is, believe it or not, a hard question: What is wrong with communism? And to a lesser extent, socialism. Most people describe communism as having the attributes of fascism or anarchy or dictatorships. Here is the right answer: it is the only form of government that takes away your freedom of choice. That is because all means of production are owned by the state. Government chooses the color of your car, the movies you see, the books you read, your health care, home, food, etc.. And to pay for this service, they charge you very high taxes. So high you cannot afford to choose going elsewhere.

You just learned something that you
will never be able to use.

UNREASONABLE FEAR

The commercial on TV says this
drug will make you feel better and
healthier, but it also may destroy
your liver, or your brain, make you
incontinent, or "cause death'. Your
doctor says it will help you and gives
you a prescription. You take the
drug and the risks involved. Then
you say you are afraid of terrorists,
so we can't allow refugees or
immigrants into America. The odds
of being hurt by a terrorist,
according to CNN, are one in seven
million. You are much more likely to

be struck by lightning than hurt by an act of terror. There are only 10-20 thousand terrorists and there are 330 million of us. Your chance of injury from a terrorist is about the same as winning the lottery without buying a ticket. If you take the drug, which is much more likely to hurt you, why won't you let refugees in? Why are you afraid? Maybe you just don't like foreigners.

MUSEUM LEARNING

From a visit to the Smithsonian:

1. Neanderthals showed empathy by taking care of their sick and wounded, and even buried people with flowers. After 70,000 years of

evolution, conservative Republicans still cannot meet the empathy standards set by the Neanderthal.

2. It is a fact that 99.9% of all human beings on earth have identical DNAs. So much for white supremacy.

3. The Smithsonian is 146 years old and still will not show human genitals. All penises in the Museum of Natural History are air brushed or covered, but I did find two (2) female breasts, on a Cro-Magnon woman who also had a big mustache.

REAL WARS

Real wars are wars between nations. We lost our last four wars: Korea, Vietnam, Afghanistan and Iraq. You cannot defeat an ideology combined with love of homeland. We cannot defeat all of Radical Islam for the same reason.

FATHER AND SON

There is a common expression: "You cannot visit the sins of the father upon the child." I'm not sure that is correct, when you look at the DNA of the two. In 1934 Trump's father marched in a KKK parade in Washington D.C, white sheet and pointy hat. His son does not like non-whites.

SOCIAL WARS

We have lost the three wars against social ills that we have started: LBJ's War on Poverty (because we can never abolish greed), Nixon's War on Drugs (because we can never abolish the need to feel better), and Bush's War on Terrorism (because we cannot defeat an ideology). Trump is going to lose his war against the media because they tell the truth and he doesn't. The only non-combat war we have won since 1945 is the Cold War with the U.S.S.R. (It isn't accurate to call them "Wars" because real wars have an end; most of these do not).

KILLING

Some people like to kill people. History is mostly a record of people killing each other, from cave men to the Mayan Tribes to the Grecian Wars to the Roman Crusades to the Spanish Inquisition, on and on. Most people don't like to kill, but for those that do, they are usually restrained by laws or culture. But if you take those restraints away, we get regular slaughters and genocide. It took a lot of killers to kill 1.5 million Armenians, six million jews, three million

Russians and Chinese, et al. Some killers can't help themselves; nature builds it into their DNA's. It is like the urge to procreate - in some people the urge to kill is out of control. Hence serial killers. Sometimes, a God is an enabler to justify killing; like Allah and ISIS; Christian Crusades. Some people, especially Americans, can satisfy their desire to kill by Sport Hunting. They shoot lions, bears, and any other available animal, even small ones like a fox. Some private compounds in Africa will... for a fee... guarantee a lion kill. (I applaud people that eat what they kill; they justify the killing.)

We will always have occasional Rwandas, Holocausts, or ISIS. We have been able to fight the killers in wars by convincing everyone that dying for your country is life's highest honor.

SCIENCE V. THEORY

The government of every developed nation in the world favors science over theory, except one. You guessed it: the Republicans of America. Our President says that climate change is a Chinese hoax; his Veep and HUD Secretary do not believe in evolution.

TAX REFORM??

The Trump Tax Reform Bill was misnamed. It should have been called the "Voter and Donor Purchase Bill". The GOP, on behalf of all 330 million of us, is going to borrow 1.5 Trillion dollars (That is one thousand five hundred billion) from China, Japan, ourselves, et al, and is giving about 70% to the wealthy, and the rest to the middle class that need it. We all have to pay it back, with interest. The wealthy are astonished at what they call "windfall" grants of many billions of dollars. They will be happy to give some of that back to the Republican candidates that gave it to them. The workers are getting about $1,000 a year for five years. Some corporations are giving them an additional bonus. That is money they needed, and they might be grateful enough to vote Republican. Especially the billionaires.

The economy has been good, and getting better, since 2014. The corporation tax rate needed to be reduced from 35 % to 21%, to be globally competitive, but that will take hundreds of billions of dollars away from our treasury, The individual multibillionaires should pay for it, not you and me. They can afford it. But they won't; too greedy. The middle class workers have not had a raise in 20 years; the corporations, with record profits, should share some of that with their workers.

IS THE CRISIS REAL?

According to the politicians and media, America is in crisis. Well, it has always been in crisis, and always will be because there will always be politicians and media. Their survival depends on the public's perception that we are in crisis. Government uses the crisis du jour to justify not funding pension plans, giving raises, or health care for the poor. But don't worry; we are hardly ever in real crisis.

Sometimes the media and politicians will create, for a large proportion of our people, a perception of crisis that is so bad that America will become unraveled and our democracy will fail. For instance, if a certain politician is elected the country will implode. But consider this: our nation could have failed when Washington crossed the Delaware at Christmas to attack the British, but we survived. The Nation could have failed during the Civil War when 750,000 Americans died, or the First WW when 16 million Americans died, or the Second

WW when 15 - 20 million died.
Our Country could have lost its
democracy during the Influenza
pandemic that killed about
700,000, or the Great Depression
or during the riots and
assassinations of 1968, or the four
smaller wars we fought and lost in
the last 40 years. All of these were
real crises. And the Republic
survived. So...we can survive one
incompetent, insecure, bigoted,
childish, dishonest, paranoid,
bullying, power mad and divisive
President. You can forget about
Armageddon for another several
hundred decades.

MISSED WORDS

Some words you don't hear in politics: kindness, heart, loving, forgiving, tenderness, gentleness, generosity, thoughtfulness, consideration, apologetic.

WHERE'S THE MEAT

Opinions and conclusions are only as valid as the facts to support them. If there are no facts, the opinion can be ignored. E.g., Trump says, "The New York Times is failing and all it publishes is fake news...." What facts do you have to support that?" "Uh, uh..."

Funniest line by Obama:

Reporter: "Why don't you just sit down and have a drink with Mitch McConnell?"

Obama: "Why don't you just sit down and have a drink with Mitch McConnell?"

Funniest story about Obama:

Nine year old boy: "My father says you are spying on us."

Obama: "He is not your father."

DNA; LUCK OF THE DRAW

If you are fortunate and are born with a rich, resonant voice, and articulation, you realize it early and work hard to improve it and polish it. Then you are rewarded with jobs as a TV host, or movie narrator like David Attenborough, or a voice for commercials, and you make a good living. If you are born with exceptional hand-eye coordination, reflexes, fast twitch muscles, like Michael Jordan, you realize it early and you work hard to perfect it and dedicate yourself to being the best there is, and you make 20 million dollars a year.

On the other hand, if you are born slow witted, inarticulate, and clumsy, you try to improve but you just can't do it. You are doomed to fail at school and at life, and you cannot support yourself or provide food, shelter and clothing. You see on TV how the rest of the world lives, and the only way you can feel good is to use drugs. Which reduces your acceptance in society even further.

It is this second group that I think government has to take care of. He/she needs to be helped, not scorned. Those of us who happen to be lucky and know how to communicate, etc., have to chip in, through taxes, to help the helpless.

This is where I get into so many arguments with my conservative friends. They assume that the inept are just slackers, taking advantage of food stamps and subsidized housing by fraud and laziness. So, when conservatives are in power, that is where tax cuts are made: programs for the poor and disabled. It is a disgrace that the richest most powerful nation in the world will let a person die for lack of money. We have almost double the number of billionaires than any other nation, (565) but most of them are desperately trying to make more money. Naked greed, rather than help the nation. And we can't force the billionaires to pay more taxes:

they control the people, (legislators) who make those decisions. So there. Prove me wrong.

FINDING FACTS

There are three distinct sources from which to obtain current factual information. (News) One is almost always reliable and trustworthy, the second is usually reliable, and the third is usually not reliable.

The first group is composed of established newspapers and magazines, and the major TV networks. Reliable.

The second group of sources of the facts have usually been reliable in the past, and most incorrect facts are mistakes. This group is composed of the minor newspapers and magazines, many cable TV networks, governmental websites and publications, and the major search sources such as Google, Bing, Safari and Wikipedia, and tested blogs like the Huffington Post, The Daily Beast, Politico, et. al. But remember that they can be biased.

The least reliable group is composed of people, groups or publications with an axe to grind, and have nothing to lose, such as special interest publications, the internet, especially social media like Facebook and Twitter, most private blogs, and most political email forwards. Any fact that you read on Facebook, Twitter, et al, should be viewed with skepticism. It is probably false, even if it says it is a NY Times article, it could be fake. The internet does not care, and no one is punished if it is false,

The reliability of all three groups can be explained by looking at SELF INTEREST. The lifeblood of journalism is readership/viewership. Lack of reliability as to factual matters can reduce both, and reduce popularity and money, such as ad revenue. Remember that Dan Rather was fired by CBS for airing a false statement, even though it was a mistake. But if you have nothing to lose by sending a false email or tweet, or creating a special interest blog with false statements, dishonesty doesn't make any difference. Politicians get away with making false statements because the public does not expect them to be honest, or doesn't mind.

WHO MAKES HISTORY

History is what man, with all his biases and prejudices, says it is. John's writings in the Bible have had an enormous impact on humanity, and tens of millions of people believe what he says. Tens of millions do not. So... take your pick. The same applies for almost all of history; be skeptical. See Google and Bing and Safari and the mass of choices of historical fact. The more contemporary the history, the more likelihood of accuracy because increased communication allows for more vetting.

The bottom line is that history may not be true.

ALL YOU NEED TO KNOW

ABOUT ECONOMICS

The world debt, what we owe each other, including nations, is 16 trillion zillion dollars. The assets the world has to pay these debts is only 2 trillion zillion. This is called a House of Cards. If some creditor nation, such a Germany, goes broke, and tries to collect what it is owed, the entire financial structure of the world will collapse. Imagine what would happen if the banks cancelled all their loans and foreclosed. This could happen tomorrow or 50 years from now. Remember, you read it here.

PLEASE, PLEASE COMPROMISE

One of the main reasons there is gridlock in Washington is that both Democrats and Republicans won't compromise. And one of the areas where they refuse to give

anything up is on social issues. No
one would expect the Democrats to
welcome a Paul Ryan who does not
want Government to take care of
the poor and disabled, including
medical care. But there is no
reason why they should not accept
people who disagree based on faith
issues. For instance, the Second
Amendment folks believe in their
hearts that guns are good for
society. But why should that be a
bar to being a Democrat? Same
with abortion: the Lifers sincerely
believe that abortion kills babies.
But why should that bar them from
membership?

I'm liberal (Duh) but I have lots
of friends and relatives that are

conservative. We abuse each other regularly, but we still have respect. That is all Congress has to do; most of their liberal or conservative opponents are good people, so why not respect them? Then it would be easier to compromise. And if they want to join your party, let them. Just so long as they buy into the party's core beliefs: Democrats: help people that can't take care of themselves. Republicans: Cut regulation and taxes; make money...

WE OWE GEORGE A LOT, BUT...

George Washington, in his final address as President, argued against the two party system, saying it would create strife and destroy democracy. Thomas Jefferson agreed with him until he was in his seventies when he acknowledged that it was impossible not to have two parties, because there will always be liberals and conservatives. Check out the ancient Greece City/States. History has proven that George was wrong. We actually need two adversarial parties to keep each other honest. GW also argued against treaties with foreign nations because they would be an entangling alliance. Wrong again; treaties are as necessary as contracts. Keeps countries and us accountable. The point is, if George could be so wrong, we don't have to treat the Presidents as infallible.

FAITH RULES

If you truly believe, have faith in something, such as the existence of Gods, or the perfection of our heroes, then facts, logic, common sense and reason are not relevant. Hence the evolution of religious fundamentalists and political extremists. (Another profound statement)

NO FACTS? OKAY TO IGNORE

Lots of intelligent people, including members of my family, think GMOs (genetically modified organisms) and Fracking (Recovering natural gas and oil from shale with high pressure water) and inoculations for babies, are harmful, even though there are no reliable facts in support. I can't figure that out, why they believe such false info, except maybe it depends on who your friends are, or what most people say.

HARD CORE CONSERVATIVES

Hard core conservatives are against everything - taxes, abortion, health care for the poor, negotiation with Iran, equal pay for women, unions, government regulations on businesses, food stamps, gay rights, voting rights, climate control, marijuana, more tax on the wealthy and businesses, more immigrants, refugees, Muslims, aid to the poor, gun control, etc., but they have no alternatives or solutions. The only things they stand for are wealth, guns, and government control of personal conduct, such as abortions and gay marriage. When they can't tell you any facts in support of their opposition, it is generally because there aren't any. They are generally very negative.

They have very little empathy outside of their own family. Hard core conservatives have faith in their choices, just like religious people have faith in their choice of God or gods. They don't need evidence. (They say they are for smaller government and individual responsibility, but look at their actions: Reagan, Bushes, The Tax Reform Act, Republicans in Congress.) Conservatives believe that if there is a problem that needs to be solved, it should be done on the lowest possible level: solve it in the City Council, if that doesn't work, then the County, then the State, and finally, as a last resort, the Federal Government. Most hard core Conservatives are greedy. They need liberals to keep them in check.

HARD CORE LIBERALS

Hard core liberals are in favor of everything, no matter what it costs... housing, food, clothing, health care, sexual freedom, equality of wealth, minority and women's rights, unions, voting rights, climate control, marijuana, individual freedom. Liberals have empathy. If there is no money to pay for the need, just pass a law, borrow it, increase taxes and or print more money. They believe that it is the government's responsibility to take care of those that cannot take care of themselves. Don't worry about the deficit or national debt. Borrow from China, Japan, S. Korea, Germany, ourselves, et al., even though we have no way of paying it back. Ignore the future; government will take care of us. Hard core liberals want government to regulate everyone, including themselves. They want government to solve all their problems, even if they could do it themselves. Liberals need conservatives to keep them in check.

MODERATES

Have common sense, can be reasonable and compromise. They use political philosophies such as conservative, liberal, or libertarian as a non-binding road map. Nothing is carved in granite. They usually have facts to support their opinions, but they are willing to give them up to solve a problem. They are suspicious of authority. They are also known as wusses. (Just kidding)

MAKING NEWS FASCINATING

If it wasn't for politics in our news, all we would get would be rapes, killings, and natural disaster. So let's hear it for those miserable, useless leaches we call politicians, who give us the variety of the human experience, good and bad. Actually, even though politicians work harder on keeping their job than helping the nation, most politicians want to make things better and do good. Very few are dishonest or corrupt on important things.

Chapter 5

THINGIES:
SOME INDISPUTABLE TRUTHS
(You know, miscellaneous stuff.)

• • • • • • • • • • •

**Try not to stay out of trouble.
(Think about this)**

Airplanes that fly backwards are worth more than planes that fly forward. That is because there aren't any planes that fly backwards. This is called the Free Enterprise System.

Here is a useful toast for events such as weddings: "May the handle of the coffee cup always face outwards in the microwave."

· · · · · · · · · · ·

Do you know how many DNA samples you are leaving behind you every day?

· · · · · · · · · · ·

Women treat their horses, dogs and cats as though they were their children; men treat their horses, dogs and cats like horses, dogs and cats.

· · · · · · · · · · ·

There are always official studies that say this or that food or drink is good for you or bad for you. Just pick whichever study you like and enjoy the consumption.

. . . .

Whiskey does not rust.

. . . .

Exposed water evaporates at 1/8th of an inch every 24 hours, and there is nothing you can do about it. So put that in your pipe and smoke it.

. . . .

My hand vacuum cleaner was sluggish, so I opened it and the dirt spilled on the rug. I then cleaned the filters and used it to pick up the dirt.

. . . .

Exercise reduces heart disease and strokes, nutrition does the same but includes cancer. So, when are we going to have something voluntary, like exercise and food that works on hearing and eyesight?

. . . .

I can't tolerate intolerance. The most intolerant people are devout Muslims, Christians and Jews.

. . . .

I am very, very good at humility.

. . . .

At noon there are not enough hours in the day. At 5:00p.m, there are too many.

. . . .

Women have to live with menopause, their period and childbirth. Men have to live with Athletes' Foot. There's something wrong here.

. . . .

One of the most satisfying physical things in life is to scratch an itch. Second place: sneeze. The third you already know. Or is it first?

· · · · · · · · · · ·

When you want to raise or lower your blinds but don't know which cord to pull, remember this hint: the word "down" has more letters than the word "up"

· · · · · · · · · · ·

My wife inherited her grandmother's teaspoon collection, some of it dating back to primitive times. You could tell one of them was very old because it was only convex.

· · · · · · · · · · ·

Our mail is almost all catalogs or envelopes with little cellophane windows. You will never get any good news in that kind of envelope.

. . . .

Hardly anybody wants to hear about your past troubles, health or injustices. Or, for that matter, your past accomplishments.

. . . .

Hardly anyone wants to hear about how wonderful your vacation was, but almost everybody likes to hear about your vacation mishaps, like constant rain or vehicle breakdown.

. . . .

Very few people "have your back" when you're down and out and broke. Cherish the ones you do have. Who would loan you $5,000 without any expectation of being repaid?

. . . .

I went to the parachute store to buy a parachute, and there was a sign on the wall that said, "Save your receipt."

. . . .

All things that grow come from seeds. I want some of those seeds for my bald head.

. . . .

Breaking news: cows, horses and buffalo are vegetarians.

. . . .

No American high school assembly has ever offered a prayer to Allah, Hare Krishna, Buddha, or Hindu Vishnu. Only the Christian God.

. . . .

No one has ever been punished for not ejecting a device from the computer before removing it.

. . . .

There would be no wars, or even hissy-fits, or even kerfuffles, if people would tolerate conduct that doesn't hurt anybody, like religious beliefs, skin color or sexual choices. (That, my friends, is a very profound statement: toleration rocks.)

· · · · · · · · · · · ·

Busy people, and lots of people who are not busy, avoid anything that makes them have to think; provocative or hard to understand articles or emails are put on the back burner for another day. Which often never arrives.

· · · · · · · · · · · ·

CONCLUSION

All the above, plus all the writings of philosophers and wise men and women throughout history, can be summed up by this simple statement created by my wife Anne:

"Don't hurt anybody, and do the best you can."

POSTSCRIPT

I CAN HARDLY SEE OR HEAR, I'M 2 1/2 INCHES SHORTER NOW THEN I WAS FIVE YEARS AGO, (AND ONE SHOE SIZE LARGER!) I HAVE HAD THREE LIFE THREATENING ILLNESSES AND SURGERIES. I HAVE REACHED GREAT HEIGHTS OF JOY, AND PLUNGED DOWN DEEP VALLEYS OF SADNESS. YET, FOR THE LAST 15-20 YEARS, BECAUSE OF A WONDERFUL FAMILY, FRIENDS AND DOGS, I AM HAPPIER THAN I HAVE EVER BEEN. IF I GET RUN OVER BY A TRAIN TOMORROW, I WILL LEAVE THIS WORLD WITH NO REGRETS.

I HOPE THAT, AS YOU AGE, YOU FIND LIFE AS REWARDING, FUN AND JOYFUL AS I HAVE.

BILL BURLEIGH
(I would be pleased to hear from you, even if it is negative.)
bigsurbill01@gmail.com

John Steinbeck

ABOUT THE AUTHOR

Bill Burleigh's last book, *"Fitness Lite"* was the first book in literary history win two Pulitzer Prizes: one for the First Edition, and one for the Second Edition. The Pulitzer Panel is anxiously awaiting the release of this book.

Although he names his home as Big Sur, California, he is a citizen of the world. Only a man with enormous travel and experience with life could find the soaring and stimulating words that he puts together to grab the reader by the throat and shake him to a realization of the complexities of life.

When Burleigh is not enjoying this highly successful writing career, he collects old weather reports. Many believe that he has the largest collection in the United States, perhaps the world. "You would not believe some of my old reports; those are the ones I have locked up for safety."

Make sure you keep this book on your shelves for your grandchildren to enjoy.

The Publisher